1

2

3

4

5

6

7

8

9

10

11

12

13

14

15

16

17

18

19

20

21

22

23

24

25

As the sun rises over the hardwoods and pines, you can feel the world cool as the dew lands and glistens on every surface under the sky. The birds sing softly while the deer graze the edge of the woods. My coffee adds a comfortable aroma to the already relaxing smell of the outdoors. There is no better place to think than...My Back Porch.

In the following Pages will be my own philosophies of life.

This is the way I look at it.

—John Henry Ragland

1

2

3

4

5

6

7

8

9

10

11

12

13 *Perhaps we are here for nothing more than to master the art of*

14 *being friends to one another.*

15

16

1

2

3

4

5

6

7

8

9

10 *When we are young we fall in Love*

11 *When middle aged we search for Love*

12 *But when we get old we need Love*

13

14

15

Look around –

How much has our ability to care been lost to the absence of the practice of love.

1
2
3
4
5
6

7
8
9
10
11 *You're growing into the person you'll be—*
12 *Careful to make the reflection in the mirror is someone you'll*
13 *want to see.*
14

1
2

3
4
5
6
7
8
9
10 *Honesty*
11 *Speaks with authority and confidence*
12 *Does not give excuses*
13 *But most of all…*
14 *Gives the heart peace*
15
16

1

2

3

4

5

6

7

8

9

10

11   *Wisdom,*

12   *when guided by compassion,*

13   *leads to love, joy, honor, respect, truthfulness and a closer union*

14   *with God.*

1

2
3
4
5
6
7   *Arrogance will cloud our wisdom and destroy our compassion,*
8   *and it can only be cured by humility.*
9
10
11
12
13
14
15

1

2

3

4

5

6

7

8

9

10

11

12

13   *Only a guilty conscience avoids true honesty.*

14

Some do not love their country
Some do not love their neighbors
Some do not love themselves
But there's one thing we Americans do love:
Our things!

1

2
3
4
5
6   *Without love life has no substance and no real value.*
7

Our streets now flow with evil, leading us blindly to our final hypocrisies.

1

2
3
4   *In these times good has become evil and evil has become good.*
5

1
2
3
4

5
6
7
8
9
10   *Some of us work from paycheck to paycheck. And then again,*
11   *some of us work from flat broke to flat broke.*

12

1
2
3
4
5 *Life takes many strange turns, and it depends on how we bend*
6 *with those turns as to how we survive in life.*
7
8
9
10
11
12
13
14
15
16

1
2
3
4
5
6
7
8
9   *There is a difference between reality and fantasy—*
10   *Reality comes with a conscience.*
11
12
13
14
15

1

2

3

4   *When expectations are set beyond attainment, it opens the door*
5   *for the destructive nature of stress and frustration.*

6

7

1
2
3
4
5
6
7
8
9

10
11
12
13
14
15
16
17
18
19

It's everyone's destiny to die, but few take the time to live the journey.

1

2
3
4
5
6
7
8   *Forgiveness is required from us periodically, but expect it from*
9   *others continuously.*
10
11
12
13
14
15
16
17
18
19
20

When God looks down on how we abuse love, he could decide to bring us home.

We fool ourselves into thinking that money will bring us happiness and peace, but in reality it is a destroyer. I'm sure someone with money would argue the point.

1
2
3
4
5

6
7
8
9
10
Solitude is good for the mind but loneliness is cancerous to the
11
heart.
12
13
14
15
16
17
18
19
20
21

1
2
3
4
5 *The deed can be forgiven and in time the hurt will fade, so it is*
6 *always a wise thing to watch what we say.*
7
8
9
10
11
12
13
14
15
16
17

1
2
3
4
5
6
7
8
9

10
11
12
13   *After all is said and done, our only true legacy is our thoughts.*
14
15
16

1

2

3

4

5

6

7

8

9

10

11

12

13

14

15

16 *The conscious deep within the mind continuously creates thought.*
17 *The only way the conscious knows it's alive is through the body*
18 *and it's senses.*

19

Mother nature has become my foster parent.

The body is the sensor, conscious is the receiver, and the sub-conscious is the dreamer.

1
2

3
4
5
6
7
8
9
10   *To acquire the ability of unconditional love:*
11   *2 spoons of child*
12   *1 spoon of forgiveness*
13   *3 times a day*
14
15
16
17

1
2
3
4
5
6
7
8
9
10

11
12
13
14   *There is something worse than a dictatorship—*
15   *A democracy that has diluted its wisdom with immorality and*
16   *greed.*
17
18
19
20

Some say that to die is what makes life worth living, but the truth of it is…

To love and be loved is what makes life so precious, death comes to all but not love.

Love is a special gift, so special that it makes life worth the struggle and gives death its true peace.

1

2

3

4

5

6

7

8

9

10

11

12

13

14

15

16

www.ingramcontent.com/pod-product-compliance
Lightning Source LLC
Chambersburg PA
CBHW071320280526
45788CB00004B/1965